BULLYING EXPOSED:

In Schools

Workplaces

Cyberspace &

Against the Elderly

"The Time to Raise Consciousness and Restore
Conscience is Now"

Shawn K. Woods, MBA

Shawn K. Woods & Associates LLC
358 W. Army Trail Rd. #140-358 Bloomingdale, IL 60108
Tel: (331) 551-8686   www.shawnkwoods.com

Printed in the United States of America

Copyediting, project management and proofreading by Cora D. Brown

Book Design and Composition by Rashaun Stewart, Rashaun Designz Chicago, IL

ISBN-13:
978-0-9899779-0-6

Contents

Acknowledgements

This book is dedicated to two of the most influential and loving people I have ever met: David P. and Alberta McCray, my Grandparents. Although, you are gone, you will never be forgotten. Your faith, prayers and guidance have given me the wisdom and courage to believe in God, pursue my dreams and NEVER GIVE UP!

To the most important people in my life, my family, THANK YOU for supporting, believing and understanding the many countless days and nights when I was unavailable or traveling the country speaking, writing, networking and Pursuing my Passion & Purpose. I Love You!

To my business partners, team, associates, relatives and friends (too many to name) – you know who you are; Thank you for all of your contributions of time, support offers and prayers.

To the tens of thousands of you who have reached out to me and asked "When are you going to have a book …?"

Without ALL of you, there would be no me! I accept the blessings and give all the glory to God! THANK YOU.

Shawn's Commendations

Over the years, Shawn has been featured in publications including:

- *World Tribune*

- *Chicago Tribune*

- *Daily Herald*

Expert presenter at conferences nationwide. Below is a partial list:

- *Illinois Parks and Recreation Association National Conference*

- *Hoffman Estates Park District Senior Program*

- *Society of Human Resources Management State Conferences*

- *Indiana University*

- *Indiana County Assessors Conference*

- *State of Illinois Small and Diverse Business Annual Conference*

"Bullying Exposed" has been receiving excellent response from institutions and organizations where it has been presented. When Shawn presented the workshop at Indiana University, he also included the city of Bloomington, Indiana in designating April 1, 2012, as Anti-Bully Awareness Day, receiving a proclamation from the mayor of that city.

Foreword

In the age of globalization, national interdependence has brought issues of bullying and the value of human life to the forefront of social discussion and policy. Indiana University Office of Community and School Partnerships have invited Shawn Woods onto the Indiana University campus on several occasions due to his skills as a speaker, his ability to relate to people, and the positive message of his platform. Shawn was the guest speaker for Moving beyond Fear: Anti-bullying Awareness Day, which concentrates its focus on the scourge of bullying, and its proven mortal consequences.

Shawn received a proclamation from the city of Bloomington Mayor's office proclaiming, April 1, 2012 Anti-Bullying Awareness Day in Bloomington, Indiana. The day brought together high and middle school students, parents, staff, administrators and city officials from the surrounding Bloomington community to address issues facing bullying. He was well received by the audience. Shawn disarmed the apprehensions of most audience members by maintaining a constant conversation with them. He was able to establish a rapport with the audience allowing him to delve into the varied issues affecting the participants. His program provided a platform for substantive expression, and offered up solutions to the identified problems. Shawn seeks to promote world peace by raising awareness about bullying between individuals. The levels of analysis entail the use of fear, coercion, and intimidation that together play a role in undermining security, while eroding freedom.

In this book, Shawn Wood is splendidly detailed. He raises awareness about how individuals, institutions and entire nations will need to transform their violent and destructive thoughts and behavior so that they may overcome the current global impasse and usher in a future of peace and hope. As everyone is affected by bullying, it's only appropriate to extend a standing, worldwide invitation to help support Anti-bullying. Individuals need to learn how to foster dialogue as a means of problem solving and solution building.

I myself found that some pages brought to life stories of people searching for meaning. By reading Shawn's book you will learn about some of life fascinating stories of people searching for new insights, new ideas, and new interpretations on what it means to be bullied and how to combat bullying with positive interactions. This book will make a difference in the way people treat students, adults and seniors. Shawn's book brings out the fact that in an increasingly interdependent world, we share responsibility for the security of all human beings. Conflict and mistrust between communities, crime, domestic violence and abuse – even the biting comment are all part of the larger culture of violence. The broad base of the pyramid is the silent violence of apathy – our willingness to live comfortably while ignoring the reality that others are in pain.

This book should make a difference in the way you view bullying. It will teach us how to view our challenges and rise above the violence. Always remain confident in your ability to prevail over any bullying situation. You will read about the personal anecdotes, research and interviews with people whom experience bullying first hand.

Shawn brings some underlying issues to the forefront. He teaches the best ways to interact with people so that they empower them rather than limit them through seemingly harmless acts. Shawn provides tools, and ideas to help combat ignorance and cultural incongruence in order to help foster an atmosphere that promotes, and nurtures peace. You will learn that when obstacles arise we must also create opportunities to help circumvent them.

No matter how insurmountable a situation may seem, Shawn urge you to hold your head high and remind yourself that nothing can hinder you or take your joy away, unless you give them that power. Forward step by step, encourage and support one another to win over bullying. Remember you all are most prized treasures and gifts to the world. Let's not let BULLYING stand in the way.

Kim Morris-Newson

Associate Director

Indiana University Office of Community and School Partnerships

Foreword

As a young child I grew up in a small town in Northern Indiana with my single mom and my three older siblings. While we were close in age, my siblings and I had our own personalities, friends, hobbies and habits that set us apart. I was involved in a lot of school activities and sports but I was also bullied for nearly a decade. My first exposure to bullying was in elementary school at the hands of a girl that I once thought was a friend. It started as verbal bullying of me as well as some other kids in school but eventually escalated to physical bullying and eventually a physical fight. The bullying behaviors were on-going but would occasionally cease when she would find other victims to target and then finally ended when I transferred to middle school.

I was so excited to start my middle school experience. It was going to be a fresh start without my elementary school bully. I played sports and easily made new friends. My first year was great but year two was horrible. I walked to school which was less than three blocks from my home. One day, as I approached the school entrance there were a small group of boys waiting for the bell to ring. One of the boys, that was one year ahead of me, started teasing me while the onlookers laughed. He would find the smallest thing and just continuously tease me – my big feet, my shoes, my hair, my clothes, my nose, my long neck, you name it. And the onlookers' laughter served as encouragement for him to relentlessly bully me. It was devastating. I simply ignored him but the verbal bullying continued until he transitioned to high school. While it never escalated to physical bullying, the damage was done. I honestly believe that those bullying experiences caused me to have self-esteem issues well into my adult years; issues that I hid from everyone, including my mother and siblings.

As an adult, I finished college and decided to pursue my advanced degree. While in graduate school I crossed paths with a lot of professionals and made friends with a few of my classmates. As I was sitting in an elective human resource class awaiting my instructor to arrive, in walked **Shawn K. Woods.** As he made his way through the classroom, he found an open seat in front of me. At the start of a new class, every student would introduce themselves and share a little history about themselves. When I heard him speak, I knew that there was something special about my well-dressed classmate but I could not quite figure out what it was. It wasn't until we had to give oral presentations in class then I finally figured it out. **I WAS ABSOLUTELY FLOORED!!** Shawn was a *talented, self-motivated, dynamic* speaker who held my attention from his very first spoken word until his last **vibrant** closing comment. Throughout our time in class I was captivated by his ability to repeatedly deliver presentations that left the class excited and enlightened. From that class forward, we stayed in contact and were able to foster a very close friendship.

As our professional lives continued to advance, Shawn and I kept tabs on one another. One day, Shawn called me and said that he had been cultivating a career change and was now providing Professional Coaching, Training and Development as well as other speaking engagements services. He also explained that he had recently completed a series of workshops/lectures on bullying for a major university and saw a significant need for more educational materials on the topic. That while the media has increased awareness of bullying and the negative impacts there was still additional opportunity to increase awareness. Bullying has been around for decades it does not discriminate and it has long lasting effects on everyone involved – **The Bully and the Victim**.

Shawn asked if I was interested in assisting with the project and given his enthusiasm and passion and knowledge of the topic I eagerly agreed to help. We readily started the research and interview process to ensure his first written words were as successful as possible. While discussing the book and how he wanted to approach the project we shared our own personal bullying experiences. While we worked our day jobs to support ourselves and our families, we also shared countless emails, telephone calls and evenings to make sure that we were able to meet the book deadlines.

As Shawn and I edited the book one final time prior to printing we could not help but laugh at our first meeting in graduate school over a decade ago. While we realized that our bond had grown exponentially as we continued to share hurtful personal struggles and successful professional growth, the book writing experience has taken our friendship down yet another adventurous path and I couldn't imagine a better person to take this ride of a lifetime with. Shawn is a FRIEND for LIFE and he knows that while I don't have all the answers, he certainly has my **FULL SUPPORT** in **EVERYTHING** he does.

Bullying Exposed has something for everyone!! Whether you have been the bully or a victim - at school, at work, in cyberspace or if you have a senior person in your life, Shawn's book has an answer for you. Even if you are simply seeking a solution to a bullying issue before it becomes a "problem" we are hopeful that your answer can be found within the pages of Shawn's first book.

Cora D. Brown, MBA

Preface

Thank you for picking up this book. I pray that the information and subject touches you as it has me. I hope that it will increase your awareness of bullies, their impact on victims, and I ask you to join forces with me and take a stand against bullying.

At a time of life when people of all ages should be discovering and enjoying the happiness and opportunity that life has to offer, they are instead <u>paralyzed by fear</u>. And now there is <u>no escape</u>. While at one time victims could count on periods of respite once they were safely away from school, work or other places where they were harassed, today's **victims find bullies attacking them 24/7,** even when, technically, they should feel safe in their own homes. In the 21st century, bullies have found a new weapon, and this weapon is lethal. Now bullies can attack virtually via text, email, chat rooms, and Facebook™; there's no safe haven from **cyberspace**.

What does bullying have to do with violence in our schools, and who is to blame?

Unfortunately, bullying has now reached a level of intensity that often results in <u>violence</u>, and even <u>death</u>. On one end of the pendulum, there are victims who choose to retaliate, and may end up killing their tormentors. Not a very ideal solution, since they have to go to prison to escape their bullies. In the extreme, they may decide to retaliate in a very dramatic and spectacular way, and that is the motivation behind such violent incidents as the Columbine tragedy, as well as other incidents that have occurred in elementary schools all the way up through universities. In cases such as these, the victims' revenge results in the deaths not only of their tormentors, but also many innocent others.

At the other end of the pendulum, victims reach a point where they simply can't take any more. Feeling that they have <u>nowhere to turn</u>, they choose the only way out they can think of—they take their own lives. There's even a term for this type of suicide called **bullycide.** When it happens enough to warrant its own name, you know it is happening too much.

Why is this perversity allowed to continue?

That's the question that torments families whose lives have been shattered by bullying-related deaths of loved ones. Oh sure, there may be universal concern whenever something happens; there's the initial shock wave that sprints through the media, provoking outrage and awakening consciousness. Unfortunately, that's typically just a temporary response. Once things settle down, everything returns to the same sorry situation.

<u>The sad truth is no one wants to be held accountable</u>. As we try to blame, we point our fingers at the bullies themselves, the bullies' parents, the victims, the victims' parents, the schools, the communities, and who knows what else. But just as the adage says, when you are pointing a finger at someone else, there are three other fingers pointing back at you. <u>Realistically, there is no one who is *not* accountable for the problem of bullying.</u>

So why isn't more being done about it?

The problem is there's not much guidance on how to address the problem. True, as bullying-related violence escalates, we've made a start in heightening awareness of the critical nature of the situation, but systems that address the problem in a focused, structured way are hard to find. What we need is a hero to fight not just the bullies, but the whole bullying organism. We need someone to raise awareness and **restore a sense of conscience**, and also bring back **dignity**, **security**, and **hope**.

I am Shawn K. Woods and this is Bullying EXPOSED!

Shawn K. Woods, MBA

BULLYING: AT SCHOOL

Each day **160,000** students in the USA refuse to go to school because they dread the physical and verbal aggression of their peers.

- **15%** of all school absenteeism is directly related to a fear of being bullied

- **71%** of students report incidents of bullying as a problem at their school

- **75%** of all school shooting incidents can be linked to harassment and bullying

- **86%** of students said "other kids picking on them, making fun of them or bullying them" causes teenagers to turn to lethal violence in schools

Bullying at school occurs **EVERY DAY** to someone's child during the hours that a child is at school. Bullying can be verbal, social/emotional or physical.

Verbal Bullying is speaking negatively of someone. It starts with calling names, spreading rumors, threatening and/or making fun of others. These are ALL forms of verbal bullying. Verbal bullying is one of the most common types of bullying.   The main weapon in verbal bullying is someone's voice. Verbal bullying is usually the **FIRST** form of bullying.

Social/Emotional Bullying is done with the intent to hurt somebody's reputation or social standing which generates emotional anxiety, stress and strain. Social bullying generally happens between friends. It can happen in two ways:

- Excluding someone and making them feel unwanted
- Gaining someone's trust and then betraying them

Social/Emotional bullying includes betraying someone's confidence and/or spreading a friend's secret all over school, damaging their reputation or encouraging others to snub, ignore or threaten the friendship. This type of bullying is most common among females, but can certainly happen with males as well. In social/emotional bullying, the main weapon the bully uses is *relationships*. Social/Emotional Bullying is usually the **SECOND** most common type of bullying.

Physical Bullying is any type of bullying that hurts someone's body or damages their possessions. Stealing, shoving, hitting, fighting and destroying property all are types of physical bullying. Physical bullying is rarely the first form of bullying that a target will experience. Often times bullying will begin in a different form and progress to physical violence. <u>Physical bullying is the most common type of bullying in males</u>. Physical Bullying is usually the **THIRD** most common type of bullying overall.

Components of Bullying

There are **three** components of bullying that everyone should be made aware of:

1. Bullying is an <u>aggressive</u> behavior that <u>intends</u> to cause <u>harm</u> or <u>distress</u>

2. Bullying is usually <u>repeated</u> over time

3. Bullying occurs in a relationship where there is an <u>imbalance of power or strength</u>

Ways Bullies Attack Their Victims

While there are several ways bullies can assault their victims, some of the more commonly used assaults are as follows:

- Name Calling
- Intimidation

- Physical violence
- Excluding Victims
- Threatening Victims
- Saying or writing nasty things
- Taking/Destroying the victim's property
- Forcing victims to do things against their will

Bullying vs. Conflict

It is a myth that bullying is the same as conflict. Any two people can have conflict; bullying occurs when there is an imbalance of power.

Five Key Findings about Bullying

1. Many children are involved in bullying situations and most of them are quite concerned about it.

According to recent studies by Dosomething.com, the following statistics were found on bullying:

- 1 in 4 teachers see nothing wrong with bullying and will only intervene 4 percent of the time

- 71 percent of students report incidents of bullying as a problem at their school

- Over two-thirds of students believe that schools respond poorly to bullying, with a high percentage of students believing that adult help is infrequent and ineffective

2. Bullying can seriously affect targeted children.

Short term effects of bullying on victims which could have long term consequences are:

- Lower self-esteem
- Loss of sleep
- More suicidal ideation
- Higher rates of illness
- Thoughts or acts of violence
- Higher anxiety and depression
- Thoughts of joining cliques or gangs

Bullied children are more likely to want to avoid going to school, experience higher rates of absenteeism, share with friends and/or family members close to their own age that they dislike school, and typically have difficulties in the class room resulting in lower grades.

The most common myth about bulling is that Bullying is not serious it's just "kids being kids." **A kid is not just being a kid when:**

- He/she habitually torments another child
- He/she takes bullying to the next level by making threats <u>not once,</u> but repeatedly over time
- Playful threats cross the line and become unwanted and unwelcomed or offend the victim
- Bullying carries over into different environments i.e. – internet, neighborhoods or community centers

3. Many children don't report bullying experiences to adults.

According to an interview with a bullied child, the victim said that she would **NEVER** report another bullying incident. In an earlier attempt to resolve an in-school bullying incident, our victim felt as if the staff mismanaged the occurrence by bringing her bully into a room with her to try to cultivate a resolution. That action made matters much worse as the bully now knew that the victim was afraid and that little action would be taken to prevent the bullying. So the bullying continued and the victim was tormented until she transferred to another school. Older children and boys are less likely to report any kind of victimization.

Males generally use <u>physical intimidation/altercation</u> and verbal aggression to bully their victims, while **females** will typically lean more toward using <u>psychological/emotional</u> bullying.

A few examples of **Psychological/Emotional Bullying**, which have long term effects on the victim and create lower self-esteem, are:

- **Damaging Relationships**
  - o Damaging someone's social reputation or social acceptance
- **Talking about a Victims Sexual Behaviors**
  - o Lying and spreading rumors
  - o Sharing secrets with others
- **Gossiping and Exclusion**
  - o Persuading mutual friends to exclude or be unkind to someone
- **Bullying in Groups**
  - o Publicly playing nasty or humiliating jokes to embarrass or demean someone

Why don't children report bullying?

- Only a small percentage believe that the person it was reported to will respond well and will actually do something to STOP the bullying

- The child feels if the bully is made aware that the incident was reported, the bullying could get worse

4. Adults are not as responsive to bullying as they should be. If there is a response, it's not as effective as the victim needs it to be.

Adults overestimate their effectiveness in identifying and intervening when a bullying incident is reported.

- 70% of teachers believed that adults intervene almost all of the time while only 25% of students agreed (Charach et al., 1995)

> 90% OF STUDENTS GRADES 4-8 REPORT BEING VICTIMS OF BULLYING

5. Bullying is best understood as a group dynamic in which children could play a variety of roles.

There are 8 possible roles in a bullying situation. Of those roles, 6 do not support the victim. That means 3 of 4 people would NOT extend themselves to help stop or prevent bullying. The roles are explained below:

1. ***The Bully:*** Start the bullying and take an active part in the bullying

2. *Followers*: Take an active part, in the bullying, but does not start the bullying

3. *Supporters*: Support the bullying but does not take an active part

4. *Passive supporters*: Likes the bullying but does not display open support

5. *Disengaged onlookers*: Spectator of bullied occurrences but does not intervene

6. *Possible defenders*: Dislike the bullying and think they should help, but does not help

7. *Defenders of the bullied child*: Dislike the bullying will help or try to help the bullied child

8. *Bullied Student/Victim:* Feels defenseless and alone and/or helpless

Most children have sympathy for the child being bullied. Unfortunately sympathy rarely translates into action.

- 80% of middle school students "felt sorry" for the victims of bullying
- 64% said that other students try to prevent bullying only "once in a while" or "never"

What Are Schools Doing to Address Bullying?

Prevention at School

As previously stated, bullies can threaten a students' physical and emotional safety at school and can negatively influence their ability to learn. The best way to manage bullying is to address it before it starts and spins out of control. While there is no way to **STOP** bullying altogether, there are certainly ways to **PREVENT** it. There are a number of levers that the school staff can pull to make schools safer and prevent bullying. Below is a summarization of the **SEVEN STEPS** that I have used to assist schools and organizations across the country in setting up **Anti-Bully Awareness** policies and programs.

Step 1: Getting Started

Review and assess the schools bullying prevention and protection efforts around student behavior – verbal emotional/social and physical bullying. The school staff and administrators should develop and Integrate bullying prevention strategies. Program components should include the community, parents, school, classroom and individuals (i.e. school counselors, social workers and law enforcement personnel) to ensure that all concerns and perspectives are addressed.

Step 2: Assess Bullying in Your School

Conduct assessments in your school to determine the following:

1. How often does bullying occur?

2. Where does the bullying happen?

3. When does the bullying occur?

4. Who is being bullied?

5. How are students and adults intervening?

6. Are prevention efforts working?

Step 3: Engage the Parents and their Children

It is important for **everyone** in the community to work together to send a unified message that bullying is **not** ok and it will **not** be tolerated. The school has to launch an awareness campaign to make the objectives known to the school, parents, students and community members.

Recruiting a speaker to come and speak at your anti-bullying campaign, school, church or community center helps validate the seriousness of the bullying problem within the community. If a student has been bullied and has a story to share, it's a powerful and effective way to help share the message and spread the word of a Zero Tolerance approach to bullying.

Establish a school safety committee or task force to plan, review, implement and evaluate the effectiveness of a school's bullying prevention program. The program should also be shared with the local police department to ensure that the audience and the entire community understand the seriousness of bullying and the effects that it has on everyone involved.

Step 4: Create Policies and Rules

The task force should create a mission statement, code of conduct, school-wide rules and a bullying reporting system that establishes a Zero Tolerance approach to bullying. These enforced polices will set a climate in which bullying is **NOT** acceptable.

> *BULLYING BEHAVIORS ARE USUALLY HABITUAL AND INVOLVE AN IMBALANCE OF POWER*

Step 5: Build a Safe Environment

Establish and maintain a school culture of acceptance, tolerance and respect. The use of staff meetings, assemblies, class and parent participation, newsletters, the school website and the student handbook will ensure that the established positive climate at school can reach everyone and is shared across the entire community.

Step 6: Educate Students and School Staff

Build bullying prevention materials into the curriculum and school activities. All members of the school staff and students should be trained in conflict resolution, anger management and peer mediation to educate them on the school's rules and policies. Give everyone the skills to intervene consistently and appropriately with a comprehensive approach to this growing problem.

Step 7: Create a Parent Checklist

An involved parent is an informed parent. Below is a checklist on what to do to educate yourself and watch out for your child.

Educate: Parents and children need to be educated on the warning signs of bullying and how to diffuse a bully behavior. Don't be afraid to set up role playing scenarios with your child and let your child help create them.

Set the Example: Parents should be a positive role model on how to handle a bully and the situations that bullying could cause their child. Ensure that as a parent you are discouraging your child from bullying activities and as a parent you are not engaged in activities that would be deemed as bullying (i.e., continuously teasing family members).

Be Compassionate: Parents need to develop a sense of empathy and compassion. One of the worst things a parent can do is tell the child that it will blow over. Listen to your child and work together to find a solution, and when in doubt – SEEK ASSISTANCE.

Get Involved: The parent must get to know the child's friends and who they interact with. Similarly, the parent needs to engage in actual face to face conversation with the child versus communication via email, text, and/or social media.

Don't Contribute to Double Edged Bullying: The parent must understand that if the child comes home after being bullied, it can create a much worse situation if the child is sent back out to challenge and fight the bully. This is called double edged bullying. Double edge bullying can actually increase the frequency of bullying.

Don't Punish Your Child for Being a Victim: Another situation to avoid is one in which the parent threatens the victimized child; or mentally or physically disciplines the child because they are being bullied. Parents may feel and communicate that the child should be sticking up for themselves. This can be harmful and deemed as punishment by the child.

WHAT CAN YOU DO?

Let the Bully know that his/her bullying is:

- Not Amusing
- Not Cool
- Not Nice
- Not Friendly
- Not Popular
- Not Welcomed
- Not Respected
- NOT TOLERATED

Tell someone and help bring awareness to the problem
- A Parent
- A Teacher
- A Bully Liaison
- A Friend
- Set up an **ANONYMOUS** bullying tip line at school

- Stand up for **YOURSELF**
  - Take a self-defense class so that you can be prepared to stand up for yourself. Physical violence should be a last resort, however; sometimes you have to defend or protect yourself so that the bully doesn't cause you great bodily harm or death. Most state laws allow a person to use the amount of force reasonably necessary up to and including death to protect them from great bodily harm.

When BULLYING STOPS - EVERYONE WINS!!!

NOTES:

_____

_____

_____

_____

_____

_____

_____

_____

_____

_____

_____

_____

_____

_____

_____

_____

NOTES:

_____

_____

_____

_____

_____

_____

_____

_____

_____

_____

_____

_____

_____

_____

_____

BULLYING:
IN THE WORKPLACE

Bullying at work can be defined as "intentionally" causing pain or harm to, or intimidating, offending, degrading or humiliating another employee.

Workplace bullying can start with a little **"healthy"** competition and develop into a methodical approach to destroy a co-workers character, integrity, credibility or reputation. Annoyances can develop into bullying as well. Workplace bullying can take an employee off his/her game, cause major internal conflict or dysfunctionality and disruption within teams, even spread throughout an organization and cause a major decrease in overall productivity. These actions can create health issues such as anxiety, stress, depression, insomnia and panic attacks. They cause chronic absenteeism, increased turnover, more sick leave and eventually loss of employment, violence in the workplace and/or suicide. People are assets and if they are being bullied at work, it's costing the company money. While the cost of bullying can vary by each organization, the general estimated costs of bullying in the work place are quite substantial.

- Leymann (1990), the pioneer researcher in the topic of workplace bullying, estimated a bully can cost a single business up to $100,000 per year, per person bullied
- A survey of 9,000 employees cited by Dr. Michael H. Harrison Psychological Associates in the Orlando Business journal estimated a cost of more than $180 million in lost time and productivity (Farrell, 2002)

Workplace bullying can take several forms:

- Verbal
- Physical
- Emotional/psychological
- Character
- Professional
- Corporate
- Customer Service
- Racial
- Rankism
- Generational
- Gender and Sexual Orientation

Verbal: Swearing and name calling in the office in an effort to demean humiliate or belittle the target. Fueling the rumor mill and spreading innuendo can create a hostile work environment and eventually develop into a difficult home life as well.

Physical: Standing too close to a co-worker in an intimidating manner or touching them in a manner that is not befitting of a work environment

Emotional/Psychological: Undermining a peer's work and keeping track of and communicating errors/mistakes to whoever will listen.

Character: Gossiping and talking bad about a co-worker to purposely damage their reputation. A bad reputation at work can be embarrassing and very difficult to unwind. And unfortunately it can easily become the workplace norm.

Professional: Consistently finding fault with the target in a public forum, talking over the colleague with the sole purpose of undermining their efforts or ignoring, disregarding or snubbing their input. This can be a peer or a boss.

Corporate: Bullying is entrenched in a company and becomes accepted as part of the workplace culture.

Managers fail to address bullying issues because they want to be liked by everyone.

Customer Service: A customer is purposefully disrespectful, rude and talks down to the service employee because **they are in a higher income bracket than the employee they are dealing with or** they believe that **"the customer is always right"**. The customer is right motto has been challenged over the past couple of years as more business owners are realizing that their employees are customers too. The employees are internal customers and deserve to be treated with the same dignity, respect and service that is expected by the external customers. Whether in writing via policy or simply based on morals alone it is the employer's responsibility to ensure and promote a healthy and hostile free environment for all customers.

Some companies unintentionally and unknowingly contribute to their customers bullying employees. An illustrative example is LuLu Telecommunications Company has a "Customer Mistreat" policy where their employees cannot disengage from a conversation with a customer even if the customer is belligerent, name calling, swearing and totally out of control. The employees are advised to listen with empathy and await a break in the conversation and then attempt to regain control. What happens when the customer is "Longwinded Lulu" and continues the verbal assault on the employee for an extended period of time? At LuLu's Telecommunications Company, if the employee politely disengages the call, they can face the possibility of disciplinary action.

Lesson Learned: Employers should make sure that a system is in place to provide the best possible customer service and also have the policies and procedures in place to ensure that your employee can come to work in a safe environment that is free from abuse and bullying behaviors both internally and externally.

Racial: Bullying based on a person's race, ethnicity or national origin.

Rankism: Bullying done by someone with more authority than the victim

Generational: Occurs when someone in another generation, usually older, gets pushed around until they are forced to resign, voluntarily or involuntarily. On the other hand, younger generations of employees get bullied by veteran/older generations because the younger employees are perceived as having a sense of "Entitlement" and lack of work experience.

Gender/Sexual Orientation: Takes place when traditional masculine and feminine heterosexual roles are compared to other less traditional roles in a negative light. This may include people who define their identity as gay, lesbian, bisexual and/or transgendered.

> BULLYS "INTENTIONALLY" CAUSE PAIN AND HARM OTHER PEOPLE

Who's the Bully?

Bullying situations can involve several types of employees: peers, bosses and sometimes the corporation itself.

Bullying Peers

Work bullies tend to believe that they are superior, better, smarter or even more attractive than their targets. However, it's quite the opposite. They are actually quite inferior to their targets and they are typically extremely unhappy, lack self-esteem, self-confidence and are very fearful themselves.

Bullying Bosses

Bully bosses create a hostile work environment. They can be menacing, intimidating and unapproachable. Some bully bosses have no shame and make no effort to hide their bullying behaviors. They may have tantrums, throw things, pound on their desks, yell or talk down to team members, use offensive language and fire subordinates on a whim. Bully bosses remain in their positions because there is no one in a higher position willing to confront and challenge their bullish behaviors. They are what we call **"EAGLE BOSSES"; they SIT HIGH and Poop LOW.**

BULLIES BULLY PEOPLE WHO PUT UP MINIMAL RESISTANCE

"Tough" or "demanding" bosses are not bullies as long as they are firm, fair and consistent. Their primary motivation is to obtain the best performance and high levels of productivity from their employees by setting high yet reasonable expectations for the team.

There is another type of bully boss which most people would not even perceive as a bully. The **"undercover"** bully boss is more dangerous and more widespread than the **"outed"** more apparent bully boss. The undercover bully boss is very cunning and clever in their ability to hide their bullying behaviors and to manipulate the perception of bystanders against the "target." Most bullies possess excellent emotional intelligence and they use their emotional intelligence to cause "intentional" conflict. They are not interested in building positive relationships.

However, they are interested in the relationships that they can manipulate based on the victim's emotional state of mind. Much of their bullying behavior is premeditated and they seemingly do not possess very much empathy.

Often times, **BULLYING** is a selfish, inconsiderate, insensitive **Cry for Help**. The bully needs to feel powerful, domineering and in complete control.

Additionally, bullies have probably experienced being bullied themselves and possess feelings of low self-worth. But, surprisingly enough, work bullies are insecure and often see their targets as having work relationships and security that they desire.

Bullying Subordinates

Bully Subordinates can create a hostile or adverse work environment as well. Say you're the new boss hired from outside the company to manage a team of individuals who have been with the organization for a while and they clearly know more about the company than the "New Hot Shot" outsider who's the new boss – **YOU**!! The existing employees are offended because they didn't get the promotion and are still unhappy about the new **OUTSIDER**. Instead of welcoming you, the team begins to bully you. They are difficult, menacing, intimidating, unfriendly and often times unapproachable. So what should you do? You have to prove yourself. You have to be fair, consistent, timely and accurate to earn the respect and loyalty of your team. This means you have to put forth effort to gain an understanding for the roles of your team members. Lastly, when things are not going well for a member of your team, you need to be a **"buffer"**. Being a buffer means to defend and guard your team from interoffice bullies and their bullying antics. After they realize that you are on the team with them, the bullying may subside. Keep in mind that the behaviors of the subordinate bully could also be a "defense mechanism" to protect themselves because of the newness of the team dynamic. Building a bond within the team is important as well. A team outing could also build and seal the bond and banish the bully at work.

Corporate Bullying

Corporate bullying (bullying by **INTIMIDATION** in the workplace) can be rooted in the environment of the organization. This can easily become an acceptable part of workplace culture. The person that talks the loudest with a stronger personality than most who also likes to push people around can easily be viewed as a **"go to"** person to get things done. However, if there are no consequences for **bad bullying behavior** in the workplace, it could spread company wide and this kind of culture could lead to:

- Low self-esteem
- Poor job satisfaction
- Poor job performance
- Higher levels of turnover
- Mediocre pool of job candidates
- No company loyalty
- Damaged relationships
- Bad company reputation
- Lack of morale and innovation
- Increased incidents
- Violence and possibly **SUICIDE** or **BULLYCIDE**

Customer Service Bullying

During a transition from being a dependent child to an independent adult, everyone will have to utilize customer service in their personal life or professional career. The service representatives' job is to ensure that you are completely satisfied with your product or service that you received. The perception of success of such interactions will be dependent on the employees' ability to "be attuned with the personality of the guest." And as easy as it sounds, the service employee has to make sure that the customers experience was pleasing, pleasant and successful. Even if the customer is ill-mannered, irate, disrespectful and discourteous some business owners have an expectation that service employees should pacify this behavior. This "business owner attitude" can lead to verbal bullying and potentially even violence.

Racial Bullying

Living in a country with every race, nationality and ethnic group can provide exposure to experiences as **"boundless"** as the universe. And while that is an amazing aspect of living in this world, it can also be one of the worst things. **RACIALLY DRIVEN BULLYING** is done because someone has a different skin color, ethnicity or national origin than their bully. No one can live in a bubble to protect themselves from a bully but we can certainly be an advocate for change and challenge the bullies of the world to **STOP** being a bully.

Rankism

Rankism is a term that was coined by Robert Fuller, author of *Somebodies and Nobodies: Overcoming the Abuse of Rank*. And while it sounds questionable that a higher ranking employee would have to bully a lower ranking employee, it's very real and very serious. It can be classified as abusive, discriminatory, unfair, biased or authoritarian toward the less powerful lower ranking employee. It does not matter what kind of spin you put on the act, it's still wrong.

Victims of rankism often times slip into a state of depression as they try to find a way out of the emotionally, mentally and quite possibly sexually abusive situation. As the lower ranking employee tries desperately to figure out how they ended up in this situation, it's more important that they try to find a way to remedy the existing work relationship by reaching out to their Human Resources Department or even seeking some outside assistance (counseling or therapy) to regain and maintain control of one's life and figure out how to get out of this horrific situation.

Some companies have an Employee Assistance Program (EAP) which is a service that is usually paid for by the employer and covers the employee and their families to speak to professional counselors, social workers, financial experts, etc. These professionals can assist the employee with issues that may be affecting their performance and lives both in and out of the workplace. It's important to note that while there's a fix for most things that a person goes through in life, this bullying will have long lasting effects on the victim's personal and professional lives.

Generational Bullying

At some point in your career, you're the new, young, hot stud or studdette at work. You look and feel the part that you play at work. You work long hours, racking up as many billable hours as you can handle and more digits in front of the decimal on your paycheck. You gain tons of recognition by your peers and bosses. And whether you like it or not, you smile and pretend to love it (but you really love your pay check). You continue such behavior gaining promotions, bonuses and rewards & recognition.

You're on Cruise Control. Your career takes off, you are able to live a successful life and take excellent care of your family. Everything is seemingly **PERFECT**. As you age you continue to climb the ladder of success. Eventually, younger and more efficient employees start at your company. They are from a newer generation and they are smart, intelligent, fast learners who have more knowledge than you had when you were that age, and more unorthodox or savvy ways of using technology and resources to get things done. They're approachable, they communicate well and everyone loves them.

The new generations are efficient with fancy formulas and functions that can calculate, correct, prove or improve almost anything. They can update, modernize and sometimes better process challenges that save the company time and money. There's seemingly nothing the new generation can't handle, or aren't willing to tackle. All of a sudden, you realize that you're the oldest person in your department, you think slower, you move slower and your most effective office etiquette that was once smiled upon is now dated, time consuming, long-winded or are no longer practical. There are whispers at work and they are all about you!

Whispers in the Workplace....

"What does he/she really do all day?"

"I really want that job...When will he/she retire?"

"How can we get him/her out of this company?"

"What kind of contribution could he/she possibly be making?"

"He/she is slow because he's/she's old!"

These are examples of some really strong comments that would be considered generational bullying.

GENERATIONAL BULLYING: YOU'RE NOT ONLY BEING A BULLY BUT YOU'RE BEING DISRESPECTFUL AS WELL

Gender/Sexual Orientation

As young children, there were just boys and girls. Boys were "supposed" to only like girls and girls were "supposed" to only like boys. What happens when a person decides that they are not attracted to the opposite sex? What was once considered closeted or unrevealed feelings, emotions and relationships have gone main stream. There are a lot of people in this world whose only desire is that everyone finds **"uninhibited happiness"** - whether it's with the same sex or the opposite sex. And there are others who simply cannot understand the attraction and are willing to share their opinions. The people who fear the unknown and unfamiliar will often bully these individuals whose lifestyles they don't agree with. They bully them because of who they've chosen to love. Some examples of gender/sexual orientation bullying are as follows:

- Name calling or using derogatory terms to refer to someone's sexual orientation

- Slow promotions or lack of acknowledgment for qualified employees due to their personal choices regarding sexuality and self idealization

How Bullies Bully

A Bully is a bully because at some point in their lives, they were bullied. Their bullish behavior has been overlooked or accepted, and was allowed to continue without any kind of repercussions. Onlookers, who cheer, boost or encourage the bully to "keep it up" through added laughter and ridicule reassures the bully that his use of poor judgment is justified and befitting on his/her weaker more vulnerable victim. While bullies are seemingly strong, convincing and resilient, they are typically weak, cowardly individuals searching for attention and validation for themselves.

Some bullies and victims share similar characteristics. Below is a list of characteristics of a bully and a bully's victim. Take note of the similarities and differences between the lists.

Characteristics of the Bully

Overly aggressive	Brown Noser
Combative	Weak
Unwilling to compromise	Insecure
Low self-esteem	Impulsive
Opportunistic	Vulnerable
Low self-confidence	Insistent
Difficult	Demanding
Liar	Nosey
Deceitful	Loud

Characteristics of the Bully's Victim

Vulnerable	Doubtful
Wannabe	Weak
Low self-esteem	Unprotected
No Peace of Mind	Distrustful
Lacks hope	Unsure
Low self-confidence	Restless
No sense of self	Introvert
Shy	Overweight
Different Race or Nationality	Disabled

WE JUSTIFY A BULLY'S BEHAVIOR BY MAKING EXCUSES FOR THEIR UNDEVELOPED SOCIAL SKILLS AND LACK OF KNOWLEDGE OF HOW TO MANAGE PEOPLE

Who's the Bully?

The Bully can take on several different roles:

- Passive
- Impulsive
- Aggravating
- Secondary adult
- Bullying recruiters
- Bully by association

Different Roles of the Bully

The Passive Bully: The behavior is typically reactive to an existing situation and is unintentional, unexpected unusual and out of character.

The Impulsive Bully: The behavior is usually thoughtless, reckless and irresponsible.

The Aggravating Bully: is one who provokes the bully to start and continue bullying.

The Secondary Adult Bully: They may not initiate the bullying but they join in and continue to facilitate the bullying behavior.

Bullying Recruiters: Can be heard saying, "Come and get some of this!" They find ways to get bullies involved.

Bully by Association: Witness or join up with the bully while he's bullying, but not strong enough to stop the behavior. They are as guilty as the bully.

Examples of Workplace Bullying:

- Threats of discipline, demotion or suspension
- Intentionally failing to recognize or reward for a job well done
- Make grueling comparisons – "my dog could have done a better job than you"
- Blame without factual justification
- Being treated differently than the rest of your team and exclusion from social functions
- Being sworn at, shouted at or being humiliated
- Lack of opportunity or advancement and threats to be put on a Performance Improvement Program (PIP)
- Excessive monitoring or micro-managing
- Being given work with unrealistic deadlines (doom & gloom assignments)

Statistics on Workplace Bullying:

- **37%** (or about 1 out of 3) adults have experienced some sort of bullying in their work lives, **12%** have witnessed bullying and **45%** had no knowledge (Dr. Gary Namie, The Healthy Workplace Campaign)
- **25%** of the workforce is being bullied at any given moment
- **72%** of bullies outrank their victims; meaning nearly ¾ of workplace bullying is executed from the top down
- **60%** of bullies are men, **58%** of targets are women and **80%** of the time women bullies usually victimize other women (According to a study by Workplace Bullying Institute)
- **25 States** since 2003 have introduced the Healthy Workplace Bill; as of book publication no laws have been enacted.

Is it Assertiveness, Aggression, Bullying or Harassment?

Workplace Assertiveness

Workplace assertiveness means that you are able to express yourself effectively and stand up for your point of view, while respecting the rights, principles and beliefs of others. It is also the one skill that can help a person effectively stand up to the bossy/bullying co-worker, an overbearing manager, a difficult team or a culture full of internal conflict. Being assertive can also help your self-esteem, positively impact personal happiness, workplace success, achievement and earn the respect of others. This can help with stress management, especially if you tend to take on too many tasks and duties because you have a hard time saying no.

Workplace Aggression

Workplace Aggression is usually a single act of disruptive behaviors intended to harm another person that occurs at work. The aggressor believes that their behavior is harmful to their target and that the target would be motivated to avoid this type of mischief. Workplace aggression creates a counter-productive work behavior and causes a lot of emotional pain and distractions which could affect your health, your working relationships, and eventually your employment.

Bullying

Are repeat attacks often directed at the target that a bully feels threatened by? The target often does not even realize when they are being bullied because the behavior is covert, through trivial criticisms and isolating actions that occur behind closed doors. While harassment is illegal; bullying in the workplace is not illegal unless it involves harassment.

Harassment

A type of illegal discrimination defined as offensive and unwelcome conduct, serious enough to adversely affect the terms and conditions of a person's employment, which occurs because of the person's protected class, and can be imputed to the employer. Protected classes in employment are race/color, creed (religion), national origin, sex, marital status, disability, HIV/AIDS or Hepatitis C status, sexual orientation/gender identity, and honorably discharged veteran and military status. *There is a fine line between bullying and harassment. The best practice is to initiate a conversation with the offender, advise him/her of their behavior and how it makes YOU feel, and advise them to STOP. If the behavior continues, document and escalate the matter to your superiors. In extreme cases of uncertainty, contact your local Department of Labor Relations for advice and distinction between harassment and bullying.*

What can be done about bullying?

The victim has to be able to recognize that he/she is in a difficult situation. Secondarily, they have to maintain a strong sense of self and some dignity. Lastly the person being bullied has to regain control.

- The bullying situation must be realized as such
- The victim must realize that he/she is not the source of the problem
- The victim must recognize that bullying is about control not about performance
- The victim needs to confront the bully
- The victim must report the bully to Human Resources
- As a last resort, the victim should consult an attorney
- **MOST IMPORTANTLY – DOCUMENT, DOCUMENT, DOCUMENT.** There's a saying, "If you didn't document it, it didn't happen!" The victim must

keep a detailed log of bullying incidents. The log should include:

- o Who was involved, who witnessed the incident take place, who was the authority figure that was notified of the incident?
- o What was said by all parties?
- o When did it take place (date and time)?
- o Where did the incident take place?
- o Why/How did it occur?

It is important to state the **FACTS**, never over exaggerate nor downplay what happened. Document the actions immediately after the incident while the details are fresh in your head.

Breaking the Cycle

A full time employee will spend 2,080 hours or more per year at work, which equates to more awakened hours with co-workers than with one's own family. Anyone who has ever experienced bullying in the workplace, whether at the hands of a boss or one's peers probably felt nervously ill while preparing to go to work and sick to their stomach before even walking through the door. *An old adage says that most employees who are tormented in the workplace usually pull up to the parking lot and most times contemplate driving by. There is another old adage out there that says most employees will suffer several major heart attacks during their careers, however; most will suffer their first major heart attack on Monday morning after awakening and realizing that it's time to go to their places of employment.* **DON'T let workplace bullying do these things to YOU!** The victim would also tend to suffer from sleepless nights, higher levels of depression, emotional and physical stress-related illnesses and low self-esteem.

Bullying in the workplace is quite costly for the employer as well. The company will suffer higher costs due to low employee morale, increased absenteeism, reduced productivity and low retention rates.

> **EVERYONE HAS SOME BULLYING QUALITIES WITHIN THEM. HOW DO YOU HANDLE THE BULLY WITHIN YOU?**

As employee turnover increases, intellectual knowledge is lost, good employees resign, the remaining employees are over worked and if the bully hasn't been identified and dealt with, the cycle is likely to repeat itself more than once. Any victim of bullying must break the bully cycle and stand up for him/herself. However, the victim must also be aware that while bullying in the work place is for a specific time of the day and it identifies your bully, Cyberspace bullying has become very dominant and will allow the bully anonymity. With cyberspace bullying will continue after the victim leaves the presence of the bully.

Defend Yourself Against Workplace Bullying:

Here are a few suggestions that **The Victim** can use to defend against Bullying:

- Stand up and face the bully
- Take self-defense classes to re-build your self-confidence, self-esteem and increase physical activity
- Report the bully and their offensive behavior to the Human Resources Department
- Overcome fear and resistance
- Worry about what's happening right now and don't worry about those things or people that you cannot control
- **DOCUMENT EVERYTHING** it's better to have more than enough information than not enough!

At some point in your life, you've either been the workplace bully or the victim. Take the "Workplace Bully Quiz"

1. Have you ever been involved in a bullying situation?

2. Were you the bully or the victim?

3. Why were you the bully or the victim?

4. Who was your bully or your victim?

5. Were you able to handle or diffuse the situation?

6. How long did the bullying last?

7. Was there anyone there to empathize with the situation and help you manage the circumstances or did you have to stand alone and fix it?

8. What kind of bully did you have to cross paths with?

9. What happened to you if you were the bully? If you were the victim?

10. Whether you received it or delivered it, how did the bullying make you feel?

11. Are you still a bully or a victim?

12. What did you learn from your bullying experience?

13. Whether you received it or delivered it, how did the bullying make you feel?

WHO CAN PUT AN END TO BULLYING?? YOU AND THE OTHER VICTIMS CAN MAKE IT HAPPEN!!

If you skipped this part of the exercise because reliving your past is very painful, go back, face the inevitable and complete the Bully Quiz. It may help to share your story with someone that you trust, face your past and put it behind you!! And most importantly, it could help someone else in your same situation or help them manage the bully within themselves.

Since there is a little bit of bully in all of us, what kind of bullying characteristics do you possess?

NOTES:

_____

_____

_____

_____

_____

_____

_____

_____

_____

_____

_____

_____

_____

NOTES:

BULLYING:
IN CYBERSPACE

Cyber bullying occurs **24** hours a day, **7** days a week, **and 365** days a year. It's defined as "willful and repeated" harm inflicted through the use of computers, cell phones and other electronic devices. The only thing about cyber bullying that separates it from the other forms of bullying is that it can all be performed **ANONYMOUSLY**!! However, any kind of communication on a computer will leave an electronic footprint and can be traced back to the perpetrator.

Who is the Cyber Bully?! Believe it or not, we all are cyber bullies!! We use websites to watch and laugh at videos where people have done something humiliating. We use our email to forward offensive jokes to our families, friends and coworkers. We use our smartphones to take pictures of things we think are funny and we post them to our social media sites so others can laugh at them too.

The Internet and technology is a cyber-bully's best friend. Bullying in cyberspace is convenient and has become main stream primarily due to its anonymity. The bully creates fake usernames and has the ability to reach a large group of people in a short period of time. Like all other bullying actions, it repeatedly and "intentionally" causes pain, harm and humiliation to the victim. The bully will solicit additional support from others in cyberspace to gang up on the target and continue to torment, threaten and harass the targets until they feel hopeless, helpless and with few options to correct the situation. If the victim is a child, these actions can lead to severe health issues, chronic truancy, school year disruption and lately the effects of cyberspace bullying can lead to despair and depression on its younger victims. If the victim is an adult, the law considers it cyber stalking or cyber harassment - and both are illegal. These actions can also lead to emotional and physical health issues, frequent absenteeism, low self-esteem, low self-confidence, depression, loss of employment or a physical confrontation and possibly SUICIDE.

Cyberspace bullying uses several different technological mediums and they all have one thing in common. They can connect several people in a matter of minutes. One on one bullying in cyberspace spreads like fuel sprayed on a fire. Layer on your friends and their friends and you've got an epidemic using the following methods of communication:

- Emails
- Cellular Phones
- Social Networking Sites
- Chat Rooms
- YouTube™, Facebook™, Instagram™, Twitter™

Emails: Exchanging digital messages from an author to one or more recipients. They get worse when recipients forward them on creating what's called a **"CHAIN EMAIL."**

Cellular Phones: Support a wide range of other services such as text messaging, email, Internet access, photography, gaming applications and sexting. Mobile phones that offer these and more general computing capabilities are commonly referred to as smartphones. A bully can use a smartphone to take a photo or video of the victim (unaware), upload it to an email, text message or social media site within seconds.

Social Networking Sites: Intended to connect friends, family and business associates, social networking sites include YouTube™, Facebook™, Instagram™, and Twitter™

CYBERSPACE ALLOWS BULLYS TO REMAIN ANONYMOUS AS THEY CONTINUE TO INTENTIONALLY CAUSE PAIN

Chat Rooms: Are very popular online mediums that will allow you to chat anonymously as well as in an open forum. There's typically no registration required.

YouTube: Is a video sharing website that's used to upload, view and share videos. However, videos that are considered to contain offensive content are available only to registered users at least 18 years old.

Anyone can be a Victim in Cyberspace

While bullying has been around for centuries, with the advancements of technology, Cyberspace Bullying has increased exponentially and it can affect children or adults.

Bullying Children in Cyberspace:

Statistics show that over 25% of all children are bullied every day!! While the effects of childhood bullying can affect people well into their adult lives, cyberspace bullying is one of the most aggressive forms of bullying that tends to overshadow many pleasant childhood memories.

Often times, cyberspace bullying can be much worse than physical bullying due to the constant emotional trauma, the anonymous nature of the attacks and the rate of speed that the repeated tormenting spreads. For every child who admits to being bullied, there's another child who's suffering in silence with feelings of embarrassment, hopelessness and aloneness.

Signs that Your Child is Being Bullied

If your child is being bullied, it's certainly not one of those things that they would want to share with family or anyone in a position of authority because they probably don't want to be viewed as weak or socially awkward or rejected by classmates. Your child may have been a popular, well-liked honor roll student who was involved in several activities until something went horribly wrong and now he or she is a social outcast.

As a parent, we are often times oblivious to how our children's friends treat them so if a parent really wants to know why their child is being bullied, it's simply because they are different. Physical differences can include but are not limited to the following:

- Sexual orientation
- Complexion of their skin
- Not trendy/cool enough
- Obese or too skinny
- Someone's boyfriend/girlfriend is attracted to your child

- Emails/Voicemail/Text messages and someone else assumes that its inappropriate

Somewhere along the line, all things good eventually fade, and your child made one enemy and became the target. Here are some signs that your child is being bullied:

- Avoids school and extracurricular activities
- Appears sad, moody, depressed or reclusive
- Quits activities that they previously enjoyed
- Performs poorly in school and has no interest in turning their grades around
- Separates themselves from their friends or family
- Appears upset after using the computer or cell phone

> **LET'S FACE IT, EVERYONE HAS THE CAPACITY TO BE A BULLY, BUT THAT CERTAINLY DOESN'T MAKE IT OK!!**

How to Prevent or Manage Cyber Bullying

Bullying in cyberspace has become a hot topic in school and in the media. Kids are cruel and some kids have been bullied to death. While there are some states that have cyber bullying laws, responsible adults also play a role in trying to put an end to bullying in cyberspace. Some things to consider helping children who are the targets of bullying are the following:

- Don't punish the victim. At this point the victim requires emotional support from their parents, friends and faculty to get through the pain inflicted upon them from the bullies.
- Don't take their computer or cell phone. It will be viewed as a punishment. Most importantly they use them for homework.
- Talk to them about next steps and how to right the wrong. It may take a while to stop the emotional tormenting but work with them to implement a plan to give them hope that it will get better.
- Document everything – save all voice mails, emails, text messages, cell phone bills and conversations to prove to law enforcement that your child has been a victim.
- Don't encourage him/her to retaliate – often times, the attacks can get worse or can result in physical attacks.
- Block cell phone numbers in your child's phone – Alert your provider and ask to block the numbers that are causing the pain.

- Involve school administrators – Your child probably spends more awakened hours at school than he or she does at home. So if school officials get involved, they can monitor the daily interactions between your child and the bullies and document the attacks as well. If law enforcement has to get involved, the school officials will become a very valuable source of information.

What's the Law?

With the increased frequency of bullying, school administrators have felt compelled to establish rules to help lessen the effects of bullying, to keep children in a healthy safe environment. Due to the unforgiving nature of any kind of bullying, children have a difficult time dealing with the constant harassment.

They feel overwhelmed, depressed and hopeless. This can lead to suicide or violent retaliation toward the bully, which has led to death of others. Before children really begin to live their lives and realize how precious life is, they've succumbed to the torments of bullying.

> **BE BIGGER THAN THE SITUATION AND STAND UP AGAINST BULLYING. DO NOT FACILITATE the "BULLY BEHAVIOR"**

Bullying Adults in Cyberspace

Unless bullying is dealt with at an adolescent age, mean girls grow into mean callous women and mean boys grow into mean controlling men. While cyber bullying is just as new for kids as it is for adults, it's still wrong and in some states, it's illegal. When adults are involved, bullying in cyberspace is illegal in all 50 states and is commonly referred to as:

- Cyber Stalking
- Cyber Harassment

Cyber Stalking

Cyber Stalking can be defined as the use of technology, especially the Internet, email or other electronic communication, to threaten and/or harass an individual. Stalking by definition may include the following but are not limited to:

- False accusations
- Monitoring
- Making threats
- Electronic Identity theft
- Damage to data or equipment
- Sending threatening or obscene emails
- The solicitation of minors for sex

- Gathering information in order to harass

Similar to stalking off-line, online stalking is a terrifying experience for victims, placing them at risk of emotional and psychological trauma and possible physical harm. Many cyber stalking situations can evolve into off-line stalking, subjecting the victim to abusive and excessive phone calls, vandalism, threatening or obscene mail, trespassing or physical assault.

Possible Effects of Cyber Stalking

Just because cyber stalking does not include physical contact with the Bully, it does not mean it is not as terrifying or threatening as any other type of crime. Targets of cyber stalking often experience psychological trauma, as well as physical and emotional pain as a result of their online assault. Some of these effects may include:

- Changes in sleeping and eating patterns
- Anxiety causing dental problems and physical illness
- Feelings of helplessness
- Fear for one's safety
- Nightmares

How to Handle Cyber Stalking

A cyber stalker may be an online stranger or a person whom the target knows. A cyber stalker may be anonymous and may solicit involvement of other people online who do not even know the target.

Cyber stalking is a criminal offense that comes into play under state anti-stalking laws, slander laws and harassment laws. A cyber stalking conviction can result in a restraining order, probation or criminal penalties against the assailant, including jail.

Cyber stalking is illegal and if a victim of cyber stalking is under the age of 18, he or she should tell their parents or another adult they trust about any harassments and/or threats. Victims should communicate that the contact is unwanted and ask the perpetrator to cease sending communications of any kind. Victims should do this only once. Then, no matter the response, victims should under no circumstances ever communicate with the stalker again. Victims should save copies of communications in both electronic and hard copy form. If the harassment continues, the victim may wish to file a complaint with the stalker's Internet service provider, as well as with their own service provider. Many Internet service providers offer tools that filter or block communications from specific individuals.

As soon as individuals suspect they are victims of online harassment or cyber stalking, they should start collecting all evidence and document all contact made by the stalker. Save all email, postings and other communications in both electronic and hard-copy form. If possible, save all of the header information from emails and newsgroup postings. Record all dates and times to ensure you have a complete log of any contact with the stalker. Victims may also want to start a log of each communication explaining the situation in more detail. Victims may want to document how the harassment is affecting their lives and what steps they have taken to stop the harassment.

Victims may want to file a report with local law enforcement or contact their local prosecutor's office to see what charges, if any, can be pursued. Victims should save copies of police reports and record all contact with law enforcement officials and the prosecutor's office. Victims who are being continually harassed may want to consider changing their email address, Internet service provider, a home phone number and should examine the possibility of using encryption software or privacy protection programs. Any local computer store can offer a variety of protective software, options and suggestions. Victims may also want to learn how to use the filtering capabilities of email programs to block e-mails from certain addresses.

Finally, under no circumstances should victims agree to meet with the perpetrator face to face to "work it out," or "talk." No contact should ever be made with the stalker. Meeting a stalker in person can be very dangerous.

Cyber Harassment

Cyber harassment can sometimes be used interchangeably with cyber stalking but differs from cyber stalking in that it is generally defined as not involving a credible threat. Cyber harassment usually pertains to threatening, distressing or harassing emails, instant messages, chat room messages, blog entries, YouTube™ submissions or websites dedicated to tormenting an individual.

Most states measure Cyber Harassment, Cyber Stalking and Cyber Bullying differently based on the wording of the laws. Some states approach cyber harassment by including language addressing electronic communications in general harassment statutes, while others have created stand-alone cyber harassment statutes.

The first Cyber stalking law went into effect in California in 1999. Across the country, laws have been passed in some states against Physical Bullying, Electronic Harassment and

Cyber Bullying. A few states have proposed laws on the table awaiting a vote while other states have had enough and are standing tall against bullying. Some federal laws are still pending but there are state laws that have been passed.

States with Bullying laws: 49

States with Cyber Bullying laws: 18

States with Electronic Harassment laws: 47

How Bully's Bully:

A Bully is a bully because at some point in their lives, they were bullied. Their bullish behavior has been overlooked or accepted and was allowed to continue without any kind of repercussions. However, cyber bullying has a different audience and lifespan. People laugh and continue to facilitate the poor judgment (and forward the text, email, photo, etc.) and the bullying continues. While to their victims bullies are seemingly strong, convincing and resilient, they are typically weak, vulnerable and lack self-confidence themselves.

Statistics on Cyber Bullying: *According to the Bureau of Justice Statistics, US Department of Health and Human Services, Cyberbullying Research Center:*

- **52%** of teens reported being cyber bullied
- **33%** of teens have experienced cyber threats online
- **25%** of teens have been bullied repeatedly through their cell phones
- **52%** of teens do not tell their parents when cyber bullying occurs

---

BULLYING IN CYBERSPACE IS NOT JUST AN ADOLESCENT ISSUE

Are you ready to take a stand and help EXPOSE cyberspace bullying?

Remember— "The Time to Raise Consciousness and Restore Conscience is Now"

At some point in your life, you've either been the cyber bully or the victim. Take the "Cyber Bully Quiz"

1. Have you ever been involved in an internet bullying situation?

2. Were you the bully or the victim?

3. Why were you the bully or the victim?

4. Who was your bully or your victim?

5. Were you able to handle or diffuse the situation?

6. How long did the bullying last?

7. Was there anyone there to empathize with the situation and help you manage the circumstances or did you have to stand along and fix it?

8. What kind of bully did you have to cross paths with?

9. What happened to you if you were the bully? If you were the victim?

10. Whether you received it or delivered it, how did the bullying make you feel?

11. Are you still a bully or a victim?

12. What did you learn from your bullying experience?

If you skipped this part of the exercise because reliving your past is very painful, go back, face the inevitable and complete the Bully Quiz. It may help to share your story with someone that you trust, face your past and put it behind you!! And most importantly, it could help someone else in your same situation or help them manage the bully within themselves.

Since there is a little bit of bully in all of us, what kind of bullying characteristics do you possess?

NOTES:

_____

_____

_____

_____

_____

_____

_____

_____

_____

_____

_____

_____

_____

Bullying:
Against Seniors
An Ageless Epidemic

The time to raise consciousness and restore conscience is now. We have to recognize that bullying is a lifelong epidemic in our society and most times is ignored or often times overlooked. Many seniors around the world are being abused or harmed and often times by people we trust and are directly responsible for their care. We have seniors in our lives or know someone who has a senior in their lives that we want to guard and protect.

While bullying has been generalized and largely thought to be a widespread pandemic within the younger generations, there is seemingly a strong relationship between bullying as a youth and experiencing bullying as an adult. Bullying has become an ageless epidemic with the seniors in our lives that we love. As our parents and grandparents age, part of loving the seniors in our lives means that we want them to be able to live the rest of their lives in a happy, healthy, safe environment – without being **BULLIED.**

Senior Bullying

Senior Bullying is very serious. The problem with senior bullying is that most times it goes unnoticed and undetected. Oftentimes dementia creates an environment of forgetfulness and aggression. It's estimated that 1 out of 5 seniors are victims of intimidation by family members, caretakers, volunteer workers, staff at senior facilities and the senior's coworkers. Additionally 10 - 20% of seniors are bullied by their peers. Bullying may not be intentional in some instances but it would still have to be addressed so that no one gets injured.

Who's bullying our seniors?

Many senior and elderly adults are bullied, mistreated or purposely neglected **EVERY DAY!** This willful and deliberate act toward our older fragile generation occurs everywhere including in eldercare facilities and daycare for seniors. Other residents at the facility are generally the bully in such situations but bullying can also occur in their own homes or in the homes of relatives at the hands of caretakers or relatives.

As our seniors continue to age their bodies become more delicate, fragile and frail and they are less likely to stand up to bullying when they are being attacked. As their bodies weaken, their minds often times diminish as well which allows them to be preyed upon by trusted yet unscrupulous people who will push them around.

How are seniors being bullied?

Most adult bullying is verbal; where one adult is trying to exercise dominance over the other. Bullying is aggressive behavior that is intentional and involves an imbalance of power or strength. And typically, it is repeated over time.

Bullying can take many forms such as:

Physical Bullying: Hitting, hair pulling, shoving, punching or pinching.

Verbal Bullying: Teasing, name calling and yelling at the senior without cause. Threatening – to leave the senior alone, to stop taking care of him/her, to 'let them die,' to revoke financial assistance.

Emotional Bullying: Intimidation using gestures or social exclusion, isolation and ignoring the elderly.

Types of Bullies

While there are several kinds of bullies, we have narrowed the list down to the most recognizable bullies that we have probably crossed paths with in our youth.

Narcissistic bully: Self-centered and does not have any empathy for others. They feel good about themselves by putting others down.

Impulsive bully: Bullying isn't planned and bully usually acts out under stress or when mad about something

Physical bully: Usually doesn't result in physical altercation. However this bully will approach you, get in your face, take your property or damage it.

Verbal bully: Start rumors or humiliate victims using harsh words or threats.

Follower bully: These bullies usually don't start the bullying but get involved to protect themselves from being bullied. They may even feel bad about what happened.

The Senior Facility

Eldercare or senior facilities are a communal environment to entertain, be entertained and enjoy the social aspect of life with people from the same generation. They gather in common areas and participate in group activities throughout the day. They dine together as well as play pool, board games, take part in crafts, workout and watch television, among other things. The seniors tend to spend more awakened hours at the facility and as shameful as it sounds, it's also the place where the majority of senior bullying takes place.

Motorize Transport Chair: Some seniors have physical limitations and are required to use motorized vehicles. While the initial use of the motorized transport chair is to make it easier to get around, some seniors use it as a tool to bully other residents at the facility. They use their chairs to intentionally run into victims and/or damage victims' property.

Dining room Cliques: In the communal dining area, the residents typically have assigned seats. Dining room cliques develop similar to a high school experience. There can be kicking under the tables, shoving of chairs and occasionally snubbing or aggravating the new comer.

These antics could continue unnoticed for quite a while until someone decides that they have had enough and confides in a friend, relative or staff member to help them cope with the senior bully at the facility.

Ten Powerful Steps to Survive Bullying

Stop Bullying Now!! STAND UP AND SPEAK OUT to defeat the bullies in this world. There are more victims than bullies and if we stand together and shift the imbalance of power that the Bully has, we will be able to Stop Bullies. Here are ten powerful steps to survive bullying:

1. Know and recognize BULLYING behavior

2. ACKNOWLEDGE that its happening

3. CONFIDE in someone you can trust

4. CREATE a Plan of Action

5. BOOST your self esteem

6. Surround yourself with POSITIVE FRIENDS

7. Try to BEFRIEND the bully – Bullies need love and attention too

8. STAND UP to the aggressor

9. FORGIVE and Let GO

10. Help other VICTIMS and become an Advocate against bullying!!

Are you ready to take a stand and help to STOP bullying?

Remember—"The Time to Raise Consciousness and Restore Conscience is Now"

Notes:

_____

_____

_____

_____

_____

_____

_____

_____

_____

_____

_____

_____

_____

_____

_____

About the Author

Shawn K. Woods is President of Shawn K. Woods & Associates, an organization committed to "empowering businesses and individuals to unleash their full potential." Shawn provides his corporate clients with up to date tools and strategies to ATTRACT, DEVELOP, ENGAGE, MOTIVATE, and RETAIN top talent. A certified International trainer/facilitator, he has delivered conferences, keynote presentations, bullying awareness strategies and leadership training to Fortune 500 companies and government and private agencies through both public seminars and corporate on-site training and coaching throughout the United States and Canada.

Shawn is certified to administer assessments including DISC®, Situational Leadership® (Hersey, Situational Leadership ® II (Blanchard), and Thomas Killman Conflict Mode®. A few recent clients have included Indiana University, Indiana County Assessor, Illinois Department of Transportation, University of Dayton, General Nutrition Centers, Cook County Government (administrative and executive), Hoffman Estates Park District,

Illinois Parks & Recreation, Monster Worldwide and Dish Network.

BIOGRAPHY

Shawn has gained instructional design experience working on leader's guides and training manuals, and has developed content for online delivery. He has delivered hundreds of keynote presentations to school officials, students and parents as a certified speaker for Monster Worldwide, facilitated online programs, delivered over 200 seminars as a certified seminar facilitator for major training companies, and authored/published numerous online articles.

Through Shawn's expertise and diverse background he has helped clients decrease turnover, increase accountability, effectiveness and productivity through COMMUNICATION, TEAM-BUILDING, LEADERSHIP, DIVERSITY and CHANGE/TRANSITION workshops and coaching modules.

Shawn's Story: Shawn is the youngest of eleven children. He was raised in a dual parent household on the West Side of Chicago where drugs, gangs and violence were a dominant part of his everyday life. Faced with difficult choices every day, some of his juvenile decisions eventually cost him several full ride scholarships to play Division I Football. With the COURAGE to overcome his difficult childhood and a tough JOURNEY ahead of him, Shawn had one of two choices to make: **1)** He could either be consumed by the temptations of the street life, which is seemingly a trap that a lot of young men fall into or **2)** He could redirect his energy, make smarter personal and professional decisions in life and reshape his Future. Shawn clearly chose the latter.

Shawn has since achieved great academic and professional successes. His list of academic accomplishments include: an Associate Degree, a Bachelor of Arts Degree, a Master's Degree in Business Administration and a Master's Degree in Human Resources. During his pursuit of higher education, Shawn was as a Law Enforcement Officer and a decorated Detective. He has also held notable positions as an Assistant Director of Human Resources for the Board of Education as well as an Investigator for the Office of the Executive Inspector General for the State of Illinois.

In 2005, Shawn developed his own Real Estate Investment and Property Management Company. With very little capital to fund his plan and a below average credit score, Shawn's business strategy, leadership and drive has allowed him to acquire numerous properties in various states, as well as partner in several successful business ventures.

Shawn has empowered thousands of businesses and individuals to unleash their full potential. Are you next?

For booking and program information on bringing Mr. Shawn K. Woods to your event or organization, please contact us via telephone at **331-551-8686**, email: **info@shawnkwoods.com** or visit us on the web at **www.shawnkwoods.com**

Bring Bullying Exposed to Your School, Workplace or Organization

In his upbeat 60-minute presentation, *"Bullying EXPOSED—The Time to Raise Consciousness and Restore Conscience is Now,"* Shawn walks his audience through the process of understanding the dynamics of bullying, recognizing the danger signs, and taking a stand against bullying. <u>Participants in this dynamic workshop will learn</u>

- ✓ Two main reasons why people are bullied
- ✓ Ways bullies identify and attack their targets
- ✓ Physical vs. verbal vs. cyber bullying
- ✓ Startling facts about bullying
- ✓ Ways to identify bullies and their characteristics
- ✓ 10 powerful steps to survive and overcome bullying
- ✓ What to do if you are a bully
- ✓ Where to seek help if you or someone you know is a victim of bullying

The workshops are dynamic and interactive, and there are options for participants to receive mementos to remember the experience, so they not only come away from the presentation with hope and determination, but maybe also a commemorative t-shirt, a certificate of completion, and a pledge card for promoting anti-bullying nationwide. If you're interested in including these options in your presentation, all you have to do is ask.

By the end of the presentation, participants in the workshop are deeply aware of each individual's role in bringing the bullying epidemic under control, and they are ready to commit to Shawn's call to action to take the Anti-Bullying and Awareness Pledge. The program is intended to help the victims of the world, of course, but it's also aimed at helping institutions, bystanders, friends, and parents who just don't know what to do.

If you're ready now to take a stand against chronic bullying, you can take action by bringing this incredible workshop to your institution, or you can sponsor a presentation for a group you support. With bullying becoming more and more of an epidemic, there's no time like the present. Here's how to schedule a workshop or get more information:

Website: **www.shawnkwoods.com**

Tel: 331-551-8686

HOT KEYNOTE TOPICS

Powerful Motivational & Inspirational Keynotes

In addition to his in-depth, customized transformational workshops, seminars, and coaching programs, the following are just a sampling of messages that Shawn has designed to inspire, support, and energize your organization.

These sessions are ideal for conferences, meetings, retreats, assemblies' whenever you are looking for that spark to ignite the flame that has dwindled in your staff.

Designed to leave audiences feeling Promoted, Inspired and Empowered:

➢ **"Huddle Up:"** Plan, Execute, Score and Win ™

➢ **"Entrepreneurial Excellence:"** How to Grow your Business/Idea into an Enterprise ™

➢ **"FUEL the FIRE:"** Motivating your TEAMS for Maximum Success ™

➢ **"Motivate the Unmotivated:"** Helping your employees discover their purpose and increase morale ™

➢ **"TAPPED OUT:"** Refresh, Renew and Revive ™

➢ **"Who Are You?"** Building and Unforgettable Brand -

-Separating the Contenders from the Pretenders ™

➢ **"From Backpacks to Briefcases:"** Excellence and Merit: NOT Entitlement ™ (Student Leadership & Young Adults)

➢ **"Driving Excellence:"** Tour de Greatness in YOU! ™

➢ **"The PEPP Talk:"** Discovering your Purpose, Enthusiasm, Passion and Potential ™

➢ **"WINNING!"** A Champion Refuses to LOSE ™

For more information about Shawn Woods' broad range of services, including keynote speaking, consulting, training, other professional and personal development coaching/workshops and published materials, please visit his Website at www.shawnkwoods.com

Career Transitioning and Employability Coaching

For professionals who are job-hunting or looking to change careers, we offer customizable coaching programs that are designed to help prepare for and obtain the ideal position. Our eight-week career transitioning and employability coaching programs are available as one-on-one, video or teleconference sessions, or as mastermind group sessions.

No matter what stage of life —whether you're just starting out in the business world or you're considering a late stage change — this flexible program will help you identify the unique skills and characteristics that give you the edge you need, and showcase the aspects that will make employers want to hire you immediately.

Our career transitioning and employability programs include:

➢ Career direction coaching for building action plans that help you gain promotions, combat job dissatisfaction, or start a new career — including entrepreneurships

➢ Assistance with selecting training and educational programs to improve employability and gain a competitive edge

- ➤ Techniques for improving your career satisfaction and overall worth
- ➤ Methods for creating a comfortable work/life balance
- ➤ Time management and goal setting
- ➤ Comprehensive services for effective job search strategies, resumes, portfolio development, and interview preparation

Choose from weekly one-on-one coaching sessions, or join a mastermind coaching group of 12 participants (minimum).

For more information about Shawn Woods' broad range of services, including keynote speaking, consulting, training, other professional and personal development coaching/workshops and published materials, please visit his Website at www.shawnkwoods.com

WORKSHOPS AND SEMINARS

Highly motivational mini-sessions to supplement your success

In addition to our in-depth, transformational programs, Shawn K. Woods & Associates offers a wide variety of workshops and seminars designed to inspire, support, and energize your organization.

These sessions are ideal for organizations looking to maintain their current levels of achievement, or for those who want to sample our methodologies to ensure a good fit before making a long-term commitment.

Just a few of the many workshop and seminar topics we offer include:

- ➤ **Coping with Change:** Effectively implementing change management
- ➤ **LEAD with Purpose:** Managing right from the start
- ➤ **Hiring for Maximum Success:** Strategic behavioral interviewing techniques
- ➤ **Motivate the Unmotivated:** Helping your employees discover their purpose and increase morale
- ➤ **Public Speaking:** Presentation skills that leave a

lasting impression

> **Time Management:** Defeating procrastination for peak performance

> **Strategic Communication:** Defusing hostility and improving relationships

> **Managing Conflict (and Yourself):** Using conflict resolution to deal with difficult situations

> Diversity and Ethics Workshops

> Managing and Bridging Multiple Generations

Our mini-session topics cover everything from personal satisfaction to executive-level leadership skills. We'll customize a program to suit the specific needs of your company, including the use of your existing terminology and directives in our presentation.

Strategically ACHIEVE your GOALS while MASTERING your own EXPECTATIONS.

What's All the BUZZ?

Very informative, Shawn kept it interesting." Joseph Popelka

"Excellent speaker, very good, I would like another event with him." Alan Tani

"Speaker was very excellent and very knowledgeable." Steve Smolinski

"Very interesting, kept class involved" W. Kilmurray

"Very informative and useful class" Michael B.

"Kept the class in with the discussions.   Used his real life examples and incorporated them with the lectures." Derek Mills

 "Message was conducted in a well thought out and professional manner." J. Lafiura

"Very informative and I got some good ideas." Joseph H.

 "Very well informed on the topic that was presented to the team. Shawn is a very good speaker, keeps everyone involved." Fran Basek

"Very helpful leader, very active and communicative and keeps group active. Knowledgeable!" Richard Christensen

"The speaker was good; he kept your attention through the entire event. Motivation while speaking was good. Thank you." Scott Hergert

"Received excellent communication from speaker, he was very knowledgeable about topic." Harold Banks

"Great speaker, knowledgeable and understanding." Al Dabal

"Very informative and great knowledge, building and tactics." Richard Llewellyn

"Program was excellent in all ways." Mike Chatman

"Very useful. I learned a lot today." Willie Martin

"A lot of life experiences and personal stories. Sometimes funny-very informative and lots of group participation and comments." Sandy Clinton

"Discussion leader was good." Stephanie Russell

"What a great speaker! Thank you!" Jennifer Sanders

"Great energy! Very knowledgeable, very good examples and life – work examples." Vanessa Bullock-Banks

"I received insight regarding people with other management leadership styles that will help me strengthen my team." Alesia Hillsman

"Informative, directed well, coaches in a manner that brings about involvement." Sharyl Clay

"Informative, fun and enjoyable." Theotis Smith III

"Great time! Awesome speaker and even better tools and information. A must attend!" Chris Sellers

"Very good speaker gave ideas for me to take back to my job." No name

"Shawn was engaging and entertaining which kept it interesting." Bi bane

"Very funny, easy to listen to, has an obvious wealth of experience and used great analogies to explain concepts." Tod Santiago

"Shawn was very inspirational and had very good analogies." Don Lawrence

Shawn was very positive, interactive and enthusiastic." Teresa Magnuson

"Wonderful work-great job, I have learned a lot." Terri Gibson

"The program was very engaging. I liked his presentation." Michael Pike

"Best presentation I have ever been to!" "Excellent Job!" Kelley Goodman

"I really enjoyed the event, the leader was an excellent motivator and very knowledgeable. Really enjoyed the seminar." Tina Brown

"Loved the personal examples-very upbeat and respectable." Lyn Sale

"Shawn Woods is a dynamic and engaging speaker. Many good insights." Maggie Metcalf

"Shawn was great, I would recommend him." Kevin Mason

"Great speaker, very knowledgeable, able to relate to real life circumstances." Nicole Warren

"Very dynamic speaker, great content, very good seminar! I will use a lot of this information on the job." No name

"Overall enjoyable day-lots of tools. Speech could be longer to cover even more content or be more in-depth. Thank you for the time and information." Cheryl Rogers

"I thought the information was very useful. I thought Shawn was an amazing speaker and kept my attention during the entire time and he smelled delightful!" ☺ Shara Carter

"Mr. Woods was fantastic!!! He definitely knows what he is talking about. I would love to attend more of his workshops." Marilyn Luckett

"Very powerful speaker. Did a phenomenal job. Thank you." Rachel Wittmer

Partial list of those inspired by Shawn

- ✓ Indiana University
- ✓ United States Armed Forces
- ✓ University of Dayton
- ✓ Department of Housing - Springfield
- ✓ Indiana Association of County Assessors
- ✓ General Nutrition Center
- ✓ Friendship Collegiate Academy
- ✓ PGC's Gourmet Cookies
- ✓ The Charmm'd Foundation
- ✓ Monster Worldwide
- ✓ County of Cook – Chicago
- ✓ Illinois Department of Transportation
- ✓ Hoffman Estates Park District
- ✓ AEI Dish Network
- ✓ Illinois Parks and Recreation Conference
- ✓ Society of Human Resources Management National Conference
- ✓ American Management Association

- ✓ State of Illinois
- ✓ Lake County Criminal Probation
- ✓ Human Resources Association of Greater Oak Brook
- ✓ South Bend Community Schools Corporation
- ✓ Indiana University Northwest
- ✓ IU Health
- ✓ McDonald's Corporation
- ✓ Gary Public Schools
- ✓ IMC Financial Markets

FUTURE ENDEAVORS ON THE HORIZON FROM SHAWN K. WOODS & ASSOCIATES

Woods to Wisdom Blog

Next Steps Book Series for Maximizing Your Personal and Professional Journeys

- Time Management
- Overcoming Fear
- Change Management
- Financial Discipline
- Change Management
- Managers and Supervisors
- Leadership
- Teambuilding
- Delegation
- Transitioning from College and Into the Workplace……. And more

Career Coaching and Resume Etiquette Book with Cora D. Brown